HERBS
GROWING
WENDY
HOBSON

Harlaxton Publishing Limited
2 Avenue Road
Grantham
Lincolnshire NG31 6TA United Kingdom
A Member of the Weldon International Group of Companies.

First published in 1993.

Publisher: Robin Burgess
Design & Coordination: Rachel Rush
Cover Photography: Chris Allen, Forum Advertising Limited
Pine shelves kindly supplied by Rudkins of Grantham
Food Photography: James Duncan
Stylist: Madelaine Brehaut
Home Economist: Joanna Farrow
Illustrator: Valerie Littlewood
Editor: Dulcie Andrews
Typesetting: John Macauley, Seller's, Grantham UK
Colour separation: GA Graphics, Stamford UK
Printing: Imago, Singapore

British Library Cataloguing-in-Publication data.
A catalogue record for this book is available from the British Library.
Title: Herbs Growing
ISBN: 1-85837-107-4

CONTENTS

INTRODUCTION

Herbs have been grown for centuries and valued for their culinary, aromatic, medicinal and even magical properties.

Exactly what can be defined as a herb is a matter for argument among the purists but, for the purposes of this book, I will use the most practical definition. Herbs are any plants that are grown and used for their aromatic, savoury or medicinal virtues.

Herbs are not difficult to grow. Whether you have a large garden or a small one, a terrace or even just a sunny window-sill, you can create your own herb garden and enjoy the delights of the fragrances and flavours of fresh and dried herbs. All it takes is a little know-how and planning and you can start at the first sign of warm weather.

This book concentrates on the most common herbs which even the novice gardener can grow. All the practical details are covered, from planning a herb garden to harvesting your herbs. Once you begin to appreciate the delights of growing herbs and their myriad uses in and around the home, you will be sure to want to go on developing your skills as a herb gardener.

OPPOSITE: Some equipment, pots and growing containers used for preparing herbs

HERB PLANNING

The most exciting thing about planning a herb garden is that there are so few rules.

You can design on a small scale, start with a few herbs and gradually add to your range or, if you have the space, you can even create your own formal herb garden. Whatever your aim, the best results will only be achieved with some careful thought.

The first thing to remember is to keep it simple. Even in medieval-style gardens in which many herbs are grown, the herbs are planted in simple rectangular beds. European knot gardens, although beautiful and complex in design, are planted with only a few different herbs.

What the Herbs Need

Different plants obviously prefer slightly different conditions but, in the main, a herb garden requires just a few important characteristics. These are easy to assess when you remember that so many common herbs are native to the Mediterranean and are therefore happiest in the conditions prevailing in that area.

Herbs need a good soil, well prepared and free of weeds. Most soils are suitable but they must be well drained. If your soil is a heavy clay, then you may be more successful planting herbs in pots and troughs, in containers sunk into the ground or in a raised garden, since very few herbs will thrive in a heavy soil.

Sun is important to most herbs, at least for a good part of the day, although some will tolerate partial shade and a few like to have their roots in the shade. Protection from the wind is vital. Cold winds, in particular, will damage your herbs, hence the common device of creating walled herb gardens or gardens surrounded by a protective hedge.

What You Need

Think, too, about your own needs in relation to your herb garden. Whatever the size of your garden or yard, plant the herbs that you are most likely to use and enjoy for they will be the most rewarding. If you are planning to grow culinary herbs, it is best to plant them near to the kitchen door so that they are convenient for picking. You also need to be able to reach all the plants, not only for harvesting but to tend, weed and generally care for them. If it is impossible to reach half the herbs without treading on the other half, your planting arrangement needs to be reconsidered.

OPPOSITE: Colourful containers in a bright position in a kitchen

Bearing these points in mind, you can decide on the size and site for your herb garden. You can then start to choose suitable herbs. Make a selection of just a few herbs to start with and, especially if you are a beginner, include one or two that are very easy to grow. There is nothing like some instant success with chives and mint to encourage you to try growing something a little more sensitive.

A Container Herb Garden

Even if your space is limited, you can still enjoy herb gardening. If you only have room for a few herbs in a window-box, or in pots on a window-sill, select a suitable window which catches plenty of sunlight and is not exposed to winds. A window-box must be securely attached and have adequate drainage. It also needs to be easily accessible as it will require daily watering and weekly feeding.

Low-growing herbs such as chives, basil, parsley and thyme are all suitable for pot or window-box gardens. When planning a container herb garden be particularly careful only to choose herbs which you are going to use and enjoy as you have no space to waste.

On a patio, balcony, terrace or in a small yard, you can grow herbs in a selection of attractive containers. Most types are fine as long as they suit the size of the herbs. Group the containers together, on walls or stands if necessary, to create an attractive display on a range of levels rather than all on the ground or on a flat table. One of the joys of growing herbs in this way is that you can change them around regularly to obtain the best positions for the herbs and constantly vary your display.

Select low-growing herbs, as for a window-box, although with larger containers you have a little more scope for variety. Herbs such as bay, marjoram, mint, tarragon or rosemary can all be grown in suitable containers. If the herbs begin to outgrow their containers, repot them or start off new plants.

Soil, sun, wind protection and accessibility all need to be considered for the container garden, as for any other. Remember, to plant up larger containers *in situ*, otherwise they may be too heavy to move once they have been filled.

Herb Borders

An easy and convenient way to grow herbs, is by making an area of your flower borders into a herb garden, especially if the border is backed by a wall or fence which provides the required shelter. For easy access the border should not be too wide and the best planting patterns are straightforward clumps of herbs.

Plant the largest plants at the back of the border, tapering down to the lowest ones at the front and position plants to complement each other in leaf colour and shape. Plants should be carefully spaced so that they are not overcrowded and have adequate space to spread. Do not, however, allow them too much space, as you don't want to end up with large patches of bare soil.

Place annuals, perennials and evergreen perennials interspersed so that you still have an attractive display when many of the plants have died down. This will also give you the scope to alter your planting each season around established evergreen herbs such as bay or rosemary.

The more space you have, the more scope you have in your selection of plants. Good choices for the front of the border are low-growing plants such as chives, thyme or marjoram. Bergamot, mint, lemon balm or sage suit the middle of the border; while rosemary, fennel, angelica or tansy grow taller at the back.

Of course, you do not need to separate your herbs from the other plants in the garden. You can plant them throughout your flower beds to add colour and fragrance to the garden.

Patterned Gardens

Medieval herb gardens were often planted in blocks, with narrow paths separating rectangular beds for individual herbs. This approach can easily be adapted to any herb garden. Use bricks or path edging to separate your herbs and position the herb garden either as a border or a separate bed.

Another attractive idea is to create a chequer board effect with square paving stones. Arrange them alternately with areas of soil for individual plants, like a chess board. The herbs are easily accessible and neatly contained. The chequer board can also provide an interesting transition from a path or patio into the garden. Mark out the area with string and level it carefully before positioning the slabs.

A cartwheel herb garden is an interesting traditional idea. Stand an old cartwheel securely on stones so that the wood does not become waterlogged and rot. Fill the areas between the spokes of the wheel with compost and plant with low-growing herbs of various colours. A taller herb can be positioned in a pot at the centre. Since cartwheels are scarce these days, it may be easier to recreate the shape with bricks or path edging stones.

Raised Herb Gardens

Creating a raised garden can be the best option if you have a heavy soil which is unsuitable for herbs. It is also the perfect solution for anyone who finds gardening at ground level difficult, perhaps because of back problems or the need for wheelchair access.

If you already have a raised, hollow, patio wall, that is a good place to start. Otherwise you need to think about the best position for your raised bed and whether access is suitable, especially if you are in a wheelchair. The same conditions concerning soil, sun and wind apply to any herb garden, so consider these before you arrange to build your retaining walls.

Because they are already well off the ground, herbs for raised gardens should be low-growing, otherwise they will be too difficult to manage, too exposed and will not have sufficient space. Larger herbs, such as rosemary, can be grown in separate containers placed next to the bed to vary the display.

A variation on the raised garden is to use a rockery in which to plant your herbs. The stones divide the plants into their own little pockets; a rockery is well drained and any low-growing herbs should thrive there.

Formal Herb Gardens

Formal herb gardens may be more the preserve of the old manor house or stately home than the modern semi-detached town dwelling but you can still use some ideas to translate to your more modest plot. Usually symmetrical and surrounded by a protective hedge or wall, the traditional formal herb garden often had a statue, bird bath or sun-dial as its central point. Brick, cobble or stone paths radiated from the centre and divided the garden into easily accessible beds in which the herbs were planted. Many such gardens included a camomile or other aromatic herb lawn which released its fragrance when stepped upon.

NEXT PAGE: A traditional formal herb garden

The potager at Bourton House, with onions, sorrel, mint, a standard gooseberry bush and lonicera americana on the fence

Knot Gardens

The beautiful European knot gardens so popular in the 16th and 17th centuries were, appropriately, best viewed from the windows of the great manor houses overlooking them. Intricate, interlocking designs were devised, always symmetrical and usually repetitive. These designs were reproduced in the garden by close-planting hedges of three or four low-growing plants such as box, hyssop, germander, lavender, marjoram, santolina, savory or thyme, kept well clipped, in long, intertwining ribbons. One plant predominated at the intersection, where the ribbons crossed over each other. The patterns were separated by paths of coloured pebbles, kept immaculately weed-free. You may be inspired to use some of these principles in your own herb garden, such as a low-growing, close-clipped and shaped herbal edge to a border.

Equipment

Nothing beyond basic gardening tools is required for herb gardening. Invest in a good-quality fork, trowel, rake and watering can. If you are marking out a new plot or positions for paving or edging slabs, you may need string and pegs. For seed growing, you will need seed trays and pots, and a propagator, or a piece of glass or plastic to cover the seed trays. Terracotta or plastic pots, earthenware or metal containers, old sinks, wooden tubs or barrels are all suitable for growing herbs, provided they have adequate drainage holes.

Buy a suitable seed compost to give your plants a good start and a compost designed for container-grown plants. A liquid feed is needed for pot-grown plants and some organic fertilizer or bone meal for garden perennials.

ABOVE: Traditional terracotta pots with accessories and useful equipment

HERBS FROM SEED

Growing herbs from seed is the cheapest and most rewarding way to stock your herb garden. Start by planting your seeds at the correct time of year so that they do not spend too long in the seed tray or pots before they are planted out. Information on individual herbs will be found on seed packets or in the section, 'Common Herbs' (p.22).

Planting your Seeds

Prepare your seed trays by filling them with a proprietary compost, or make your own with five parts good topsoil, two parts grit or perlite, two parts washed sharp sand and three parts moss peat. This will provide the seeds with a good growing medium that has adequate moisture retention and circulation of air. Spread the compost evenly, level the top then water thoroughly and allow to drain. Seed trays with individual compartments are widely available and if you use these you may avoid the need for potting on.

There are two methods of sewing the seeds in undivided trays. You can broadcast the seeds, which means that you sprinkle the seeds evenly across the surface of the compost. Alternatively, you can use a fine cane or pencil and gently press it into the compost to make fine drills in which to sprinkle the seeds. If you have divided trays, press one or two seeds into each section. Crumble or sieve enough fine compost to cover the seeds to about twice their diameter. Water them lightly or spray the surface of the compost with a plant spray.

Place the seed trays in a light, warm place, for example on an indoor window-sill or in a greenhouse, away from direct sunlight. Cover them with a propagator lid, a piece of glass, or a sheet of plastic.

If you have nowhere under cover to keep your seed trays, leave the planting for a few weeks until the weather is warmer, then position the trays against a warm, sunny wall and cover them carefully to retain moisture and heat.

The covering will help the compost to retain moisture while the seeds are germinating but you should check the trays each day to ensure that the compost remains moist. Press the compost gently with your finger rather than relying on its appearance; a peat-based compost may still look damp when it has already dried out.

As soon as the seedlings begin to emerge from the soil, remove the cover. The first leaves are the seed leaves which are quite different from the eventual leaves of the herb plant. Once the second set of leaves appear, they will be recognizable as those of the variety of herb you have planted. Keep the seedlings moist and in good light (but not direct sunlight) so that they grow short and stocky.

Potting On

Once the seedlings have developed several sets of leaves they will have adequate root systems to stand transplanting into larger pots.

Fill small pots with compost, water them thoroughly and leave to drain. Gently lift a batch of seedlings from the seed tray and, holding them by the leaves not the stems which are easily squashed, separate the seedlings carefully. Make a hole in the centre of the compost with your finger or a dibber, lower in the seedling until the first leaves are level with the compost and firm the compost gently around the roots.

Keep the herbs in a warm, sunny spot but not in strong sunlight; water them regularly but take care not to allow them to become waterlogged. Standing the pots on a tray of gravel is a good way to maintain the correct drainage.

Hardening Off and Planting Out

By the time the herbs have developed into sturdy little plants, the weather should be warmer and the danger of frosts gone. Place the pots outside during the day, bringing them in at night until the weather is warm enough for them to be planted out. If you are not quite sure where to position them in the garden or yard, stand the pots on the soil for a day or so until you decide.

Make sure the soil is well dug and free of weeds. Dig a hole slightly larger than the pot. Holding your hand over the top of the earth, turn the pot upside-down and gently squeeze or tap the pot to release the herb with its root ball complete. Place the plant in the hole so that the top of the earth is level with the top of the earth from the pot. Fill in and gently press the soil down around the plant and water it daily for a few days until it is established. Use the same technique if you are planting herbs that you have bought from the nursery or garden centre.

Sowing Directly into the Garden

Many herbs can be planted directly in their growing positions, although you will generally need to wait for the warmer weather to arrive.

Prepare the ground by clearing any weeds and raking the soil until it is fine and crumbly. Press the handle of a rake along the soil to make a drill, then scatter the seeds along the drill or broadcast them across the raked soil. Crumble some fine earth over the seeds to cover them lightly. Water the seed bed and if the weather is dry continue to water regularly until the seeds germinate. Thin the seedlings out, if necessary.

OPPOSITE: Small pots with seedlings in a warm light area on a tray of gravel

HERB CUTTINGS

Some herbs may be successfully propagated by stem or root cuttings, or by dividing existing plants.

STEM CUTTINGS

Stem cuttings can be taken from established perennial plants such as rosemary and lavender at any time while they are growing. Stem cuttings should not be taken from plants when they are dormant.

Using a sharp knife, cut off the ends of non-flowering shoots just below a set of leaves so that the cuttings are about 10 cm/4 inches long. Remove all the leaves from the bottom of the stems and dip in hormone powder, if you wish. Press the cuttings into a seed tray or pots containing well-watered compost and place in a warm spot, shaded from direct sun. You can cover the trays with polythene, but make sure you keep it well clear of the cuttings.

Ensure that the cuttings are adequately watered as the roots develop, which will take between three and six weeks. Some plants need heat below the soil to encourage the roots to form and you can provide this with special heating cables, available from specialist nurseries and garden centres.

Once the roots have developed, new leaves will start to show. Uncover the plants, pinch out the tops and leave them in a warm place until they are well established and ready to be planted out (p.14).

ROOT CUTTINGS

Root cuttings can be taken from herbs such as mint that send up new shoots from the roots around the main plant. At the end of the growing season, cut off sections of the root and place just beneath the surface of some well-watered and drained compost in a seed tray or pot. Cover with a plastic lid and leave outside in all but the coldest areas. Remove the covering once the roots begin to shoot and plant out when well established (p.14).

DIVIDING EXISTING PLANTS

Some perennial herbs, such as chives, can be propagated by dividing existing plants. Lift the whole plant from the soil with a fork, taking care to keep the root ball intact. For some plants, you will be able to tease the roots apart into clumps using your fingers. Plants with a dense root ball will need to be divided by pushing two forks into the centre of the clump, both facing outwards, and prise the clump apart. Replant in well-prepared, well-watered soil.

HERB CARE

If you have planted your herbs with care, they should need little attention to keep them healthy.

Make sure they are properly spaced so they have sufficient light and air; they will thrive under these conditions and diseases will be less likely to spread. Keep the ground weed-free by regular hoeing and nip out the tops of herbs or trim them back to encourage bushy growth.

Garden herbs will not generally need feeding but you can encourage perennial herbs with a sprinkling of bone meal or organic fertilizer at the beginning of the growing season.

At the end of the season, clear away any herbs that have died back. Mark the position of any perennial herbs which die back in the winter so that you do not sow seed over them by mistake.

Most common herbs should be trouble-free. If any are infested with greenfly or aphids, spray them with a natural insecticide, following the instructions on the bottle. Plants which are badly infested are best destroyed before they begin to affect healthy specimens.

For care of container-grown herbs, the information will be found in the next chapter (p.18).

Harvesting

Snip off fresh herb leaves or sprigs throughout the season for use in the kitchen.

For drying, leaves or sprigs should be picked on a dry day before the plant flowers as, once the flowers appear, the leaves become less aromatic. Pick flowers for drying early in the morning on a dry day when they have just fully opened. Collect seed heads when the seeds are ripe and brown. Lift roots in the autumn.

HERBS IN POTS

Many herbs can be grown in containers, so you can create a herb garden in pots on a patio, terrace, in a small yard or even in a window-box.

BUYING HERBS IN POTS

Most garden centres stock a good selection of pot-grown herbs. If you do not have the space to grow all or even any of your plants from seed, want to create your herb garden quickly or add established plants to your range, this is a good way to start.

Since this is the most expensive source, decide on the herbs you wish to buy before you visit the shop or nursery so that you will not be tempted to buy more than you have room for. Also, pick the correct time of year to buy the herbs so that they can be planted directly in the soil or in suitable containers.

Go to a reputable nursery or garden centre. Look for herbs which have been planted singly rather than several small plants in one pot; they may look bushy planted in this way, but the individual plants will not be as healthy. If plants have been forced in a greenhouse, or if they have received insufficient light, they will be tall and leggy and the leaves will have a pale appearance. Leave those on the shelf, too. Choose small, bushy, strong-looking plants which are not in flower and which have healthy, bright coloured leaves. They should be free from disease or insect pests and should not have roots growing out of the drainage holes in the pot, which indicates that they have been potted up for too long. Bring the plants home, place them in a shady spot and water them thoroughly. If you are planting them out in the garden, use the same technique as you would for planting out home-grown herbs (p.14).

Growing Herbs Indoors

To grow herbs indoors successfully, you need to find a sunny spot away from draughts where the temperature is evenly maintained. Unfortunately, the kitchen is not always the ideal place as the temperature tends to vary considerably. Use a compost for indoor plants in pots with a diameter of about half the height of the plant. Stand the pots on trays or saucers of gravel.

Growing Herbs in Pots and Containers

For container gardens, the herb can remain in its original pot if it is sufficiently large. Stand the pots on a saucer or tray of gravel so that they can be watered regularly but can drain well. Position them where they gain plenty of light, grouping them attractively.

Window-boxes or troughs need to be about 25 cm/10 inches deep. Line the base with broken crocks, pieces of terracotta or stones to cover the drainage holes then add some manure to maintain the moisture. Layer some compost in the box or trough. Position the herbs carefully, ensuring that they are properly spaced, then fill with compost, levelling the surface. Water thoroughly and drain well.

Large terracotta pots with side holes for a variety of herbs can be an attractive option for low-growing herbs. Fill the pot with compost and plant the separate holes individually. Position larger containers before you fill them, otherwise. they will be too heavy to move.

Herbs will grow well in hanging baskets lined with moss or a sponge or compressed card liner. Sprinkle some compost in the base of the basket then position the herbs and fill with compost, pressing down gently. Parsley makes an attractive display, especially if planted with a pelargonium or other colourful flowering plant. Hang the basket in an easily accessible position outside the kitchen window.

Caring for Container-Grown Herbs

Herbs grown in containers, whether indoors or out, will need checking daily and watering regularly. They will also need to be fed with a liquid feed mixed in water every week or so. Indoor plants will need a regular spray of lukewarm water to keep the leaves clean and maintain the humidity. They will also benefit from a few hours in the fresh air on sunny, warm days. Turn pots which have side holes regularly so that all the herbs gain a share of the sunlight.

Repot plants if they become too large for their container, or once a year to give them a fresh supply of nutrients. To repot, choose a pot slightly larger than the existing pot, put a few broken crocks or pebbles in the bottom and a little fresh compost. Tip the herb out of its pot and shake off any loose soil. Put the herb into the new pot and fill the sides with fresh compost. Water it thoroughly and leave it to drain.

NEXT PAGE: A collection of attractive containers for growing herbs

COMMON HERBS

This section provides all the information you need to grow a range of useful herbs. However, since space is limited, only the most popular herbs have been included.

Some useful herbs, such as nettle, dandelion or elder, can be collected from the hedgerow or grown in a wild area at the back of the garden. Others, such as rose, nasturtium or marigold, will be part of your flower border, while culinary herbs such as garlic can either be home-grown or purchased.

All these herbs can be grown in a temperate climate. While hardy herbs will survive most winters, half-hardy herbs will need to be protected during the coldest months. Tender plants will not survive the winter.

Perennials grow up every year, although they may die back in winter. Biennials grow from seed in one year then flower and die back the following year. Annuals grow from seed, flower and die within one season.

Herbal remedies are among the oldest medicines and have been used successfully for thousands of years. A few of the main medicinal uses of the herbs have been included but herbal medicine is the preserve of the qualified practitioner; if the subject interests you, seek professional advice.

NOTE: MEDICINAL USES:

The medicinal uses of herbs in this book are given as a guide and should not be used instead of any prescribed medicine. Although they are natural and generally harmless, care should be taken when using herbs for any medicinal purposes.

Do not use if you are pregnant, without advice from your doctor. If any allergic reactions occur stop using the herb immediately and if the symptoms persist consult your doctor.

Angelica

(angelica archangelica)

Most commonly found candied and baked in cakes, an angel is supposed to have recommended angelica to a monk to alleviate the suffering of plague victims.

Type:	Hardy biennial.
Description:	A tall plant, up to 1.5 metres/5 feet, with large, bright green leaves, the heads of greenish-white flowers form in mid to late summer.
Conditions:	Sun or partial shade in a humus-rich soil.
How to grow:	Sow fresh seeds in seed trays in early spring or late summer to overwinter in a greenhouse, or lift the seedlings from around an established plant in spring or autumn. Plant out seedlings when small to about 60 cm/2 feet apart.
How to preserve:	Dry leaves or cut young stems from established plants in their second spring.
Main uses:	Candied angelica is used in cakes and preserves. The chopped fresh leaves can be added to stewed fruit to reduce tartness and are used to flavour liqueurs. In some countries, stems and roots are eaten raw. Commercial oils from the seeds and roots are used for cosmetics.
Medicinal uses:	To treat minor skin problems and combat flatulence and dyspepsia.

Basil

(ocimum basilicum)

Originally from the Pacific Islands, basil spread to Asia and then Europe and beyond in the 16th century. It is most widely used in the Mediterranean, where it is an essential ingredient in many dishes and also a symbol of fertility.

Type:	Half-hardy annual.
Description:	A highly aromatic herb about 23 cm/9 inches tall with shiny, dark green leaves and small white flowers in mid summer which are attractive to bees.
Conditions:	Full sun in a rich, weed-free soil.
How to grow:	Sow in seed trays in early spring or directly in the garden in late spring, then plant out 15 cm/ 6 inches apart. Cut off the flower heads to promote leaf growth. Cut the leaves throughout the growing season. Suitable for containers; if planted in late summer, basil will grow into the winter.
How to preserve:	Dry or freeze leaves or preserve in vinegar or oil.
Main uses:	Essential in Mediterranean cooking, basil is used in salads, soups and casseroles with tomatoes, fish, chicken and lamb.
Medicinal uses:	As a tonic against rheumatism, to counteract flatulence and ease stomach pains.

OPPOSITE: Basil used in a simple basic salad

Bay

(laurus nobilis)

The most famous use of bay is for the wreaths given to victors and heroes as the symbol of the god Apollo in Ancient Rome.

Type: Hardy evergreen.

Description: A compact bush up to 3 metres/10 feet tall with glossy, oval leaves, bright green when new, then darkening. Small, yellowish, fluffy flowers bloom in spring.

Conditions: Full sun and protection from the wind in a rich, well-drained soil.

How to grow: Buy a plant or take stem cuttings in spring from the bottom half of an established plant. Cuttings need heat from below, are slow to root and must be kept a year before planting out. Protect from frost. Suitable for containers.

How to preserve: Dry leaves.

Main uses: Used to flavour all kinds of marinades, stocks, soups, casseroles and terrines, bay is an essential ingredient in *bouquet garni* with parsley and thyme. It is also used for milk puddings.

Medicinal uses: Good for the stomach and used externally to treat sprains, bruises and rheumatism.

ABOVE: Bay leaves

Bergamot

(monarda didyma)

A native of South America and parts of North America, bergamot is a bold and attractive plant with a wonderful fragrance.

Type:	Hardy perennial.
Description:	Bergamot grows in large clumps about 90 cm/3 feet tall. Its leaves are hairy and the bright scarlet, spiky flowers appear throughout the summer and attract bees and insects.
Conditions:	Sun with shaded roots in a moist soil.
How to grow:	Sow in seed trays in early spring. Take stem cuttings or rooted pieces from the edges of established plants in spring and plant out 30 cm/12 inches apart. Divide and replant clumps every few years as the centres tend to die back.
How to preserve:	Dry leaves and flowers.
Main uses:	Fresh or dried leaves are used in teas, jellies and drinks, while young leaves are used in salads and are good served with pork. Dried leaves and flowers are excellent for pot-pourri.
Medicinal uses:	Good for the digestion, bergamot is also used as an antiseptic and to combat colds.

Borage

(borago officinalis)

It was the Ancient Romans who first floated borage flowers in cups of wine. Originally from Aleppo in Syria, borage was believed to drive away sadness.

Type:	Hardy annual.
Description:	On tall, prickly stems about 45 cm/18 inches high, the large, rather limp-looking, serrated leaves are pale green and covered with soft hairs. Sprays of pendulous blue, star-shaped flowers appear gradually from mid summer until the weather turns cold, attracting bees and other insects.
Conditions:	Sun in a light, well-drained soil.
How to grow:	Make successive sowings in seed trays from early spring, then plant out when small seedlings 45 cm/18 inches apart, or sow directly in the garden. Plants may self-seed and seedlings will survive a mild winter. Suitable for containers.
How to preserve:	Dry or freeze leaves or flowers.
Main uses:	Best fresh, the flowers are used to garnish and flavour salads and drinks with a mild, cucumber-like taste. The leaves are used to make a hot or cold tea or may be added to salads; the stems can be candied. Flowers can be frozen in ice cubes to decorate summer drinks.
Medicinal uses:	To treat skin disease, bruises and inflammation, as well as stress, colds, fevers, lung complaints and rheumatism.

OPPOSITE: Roman camomile

Camomile, Roman

(chamaemelum nobile)

Camomile has always been highly regarded in herbal medicine. It has an apple-like fragrance and is often planted to create aromatic lawns. There are two types, this perennial and German camomile (*matricaria recutita*) an annual plant that can be grown from seed. Their qualities are similar.

Type:	Hardy perennial.
Description:	About 30 cm/12 inches high, Roman camomile has bright green, feathery leaves and white daisy flowers with a yellow centre which bloom throughout the summer.
Conditions:	Full sun in a well-drained soil.
How to grow:	Cut off and plant side shoots outside in early spring. Can also be grown from seed.
How to preserve:	Dry flowers.
Main uses:	Scented lawns, herbal teas, cosmetics and hair preparations are the most common uses of camomile.
Medicinal uses:	To combat headaches and migraine, toothache, earache and neuralgia and as a general tonic or a poultice for swellings.

Caraway

(carum carvi)

The dainty heads of white caraway flowers are supposed to prevent lovers from wandering.

Type:	Hardy biennial.
Description:	Caraway grows to about 30 cm/3 feet high with thin, feathery leaves. Tufts of white flowers bloom in spring.
Conditions:	Full sun in a rich soil.
How to grow:	Sow seed directly in the garden in late summer, then thin out to 20 cm/8 inches. Plants will die back then grow and flower the following year.
How to preserve:	Dry ripe seeds in mid summer.
Main uses:	Seeds are added to breads and cakes and fresh leaves can be used in salads and soups. The roots are sometimes cooked as a root vegetable.
Medicinal uses:	To ease stomach upsets, dyspepsia and throat infections and to prevent colds.

ABOVE: Caraway seeds used in cake baking

CHERVIL

(anthriscus cerefolium)

Brought from the Levant and the Mediterranean, chervil is sometimes called 'gourmet's parsley'.

TYPE:	Hardy annual.
DESCRIPTION:	Chervil grows to about 45 cm/18 inches and has small, feathery, fern-like leaves and umbels of tiny white flowers in summer.
CONDITIONS:	Partial shade in a moist soil.
HOW TO GROW:	Make successive sowings directly in the garden from early spring, then thin out to 15 cm/6 inches apart. Pick leaves regularly to encourage new growth.
HOW TO PRESERVE:	Dry leaves and store in a dark place.
MAIN USES:	Essential for *fines herbes*, chervil is also used in egg and fish dishes, sauces, salads and butters.
MEDICINAL USES:	As a diuretic and stimulant and to lower blood pressure.

NEXT PAGE: Chives and cheese

CHIVES

(allium schoenoprasum)

One of the most common herbs and very easy to grow, this relation of the onion is a must even in the smallest herb garden.

TYPE:	Hardy perennial.
DESCRIPTION:	Chives grow in small clumps and have hollow, grass-like stems. The purple flowers resemble spiky balls.
CONDITIONS:	Sun or partial shade in a moist soil.
HOW TO GROW:	Sow in seed trays in spring or autumn, then plant in batches 15 cm/6 inches apart. Lift and divide clumps every three years in autumn. Trim regularly. Suitable for containers.
HOW TO PRESERVE:	Freeze leaves or dry flower heads.
MAIN USES:	Chives add a mild onion flavour to *fines herbes*, egg, cheese or vegetable dishes, soups or salads. Flower heads can be used to garnish consommé or other soups or to decorate cheese boards.
MEDICINAL USES:	Although chives are good for the appetite, garlic is generally preferred medicinally.

Comfrey

(symphytum officinale)

Comfrey is believed to have been brought back from the Middle East by crusaders who found it effective in helping battle wounds to heal, hence some of its common names: knitbone, knitback and boneset. It was even thought to have miraculous qualities.

Type:	Hardy perennial.
Description:	Growing to about 75 cm/212 feet on hollow, hairy stems, comfrey has large, hairy leaves. The white or lilac flowers dangle in clusters on arched stems in summer.
Conditions:	Sun or partial shade in a moist, well-drained soil.
How to grow:	Divide roots in spring and plant out 60 cm/2 feet apart. Seeds can be planted directly in the garden in spring but are slow to grow.
How to preserve:	Dry leaves or roots in spring.
Main uses:	Comfrey has disinfectant qualities and is sometimes used in cosmetics.
Medicinal uses:	A valuable medicinal herb used to treat bruises or skin problems, broken bones, rheumatic pain and arthritis.

CORIANDER (CILANTRO)

(coriandrum sativum)

Coriander (cilantro) was cultivated by the Ancient Egyptians and both leaves and seeds have been used for thousands of years.It will be less pungent than imported varieties grown in temperate regions.

TYPE:	Hardy annual.
DESCRIPTION:	This herb can grow to 60 cm/2 feet tall and has bright green leaves, fan-like at the bottom and filigree at the top. Tiny lilac flowers attract insects in summer.
CONDITIONS:	Sun in a moist soil.
HOW TO GROW:	Make successive sowings directly in the garden from spring onwards, then thin out to 20 cm/ 8 inches apart. Stake up if necessary. Suitable for containers.
HOW TO PRESERVE:	Dry ripe seeds. Preserve leaves in oil or vinegar.
MAIN USES:	Both seeds and leaves are common in Asian and Middle Eastern dishes such as curries, spicy sauces and chutneys.
MEDICINAL USES:	Mainly a culinary herb but considered good for the digestion.

ABOVE: Coriander (Cilantro) used in Eastern dishes

Dill

(anethum graveolens)

Best known for its use in Scandinavian and Central European cooking, dill's popularity as a culinary herb is increasing.

Type:	Hardy annual.
Description:	A tall plant with hollow stems, 90 cm/3 feet high, dill has feathery, blue-green, finely-cut leaves and tiny yellow flowers in mid summer.
Conditions:	Sun and shelter from winds in a loose, rich soil.
How to grow:	Make successive sowings directly in the garden from spring onwards, then thin out to 30 cm/ 12 inches apart. Dill will self-seed.
How to preserve:	Dry ripe seeds. Dry flowers for arrangements. Freeze leaves or flower heads. Preserve seeds and leaves in vinegar and flower heads in oil.
Main uses:	Fresh leaves are used to flavour salmon and potatoes. The seeds and leaves are used in pickles and vinegar, as a garnish for vegetables and in cream or soured cream sauces.
Medicinal uses:	As an aid to digestion and in gripe water.

ABOVE: Dill has a range of culinary uses

FENNEL

(foeniculum vulgare)

Brought to Roman Britain, fennel was stuffed into keyholes to stop evil spirits in the Middle Ages. The seeds were nibbled by congregations to stave off hunger during Puritan services in the United States.

TYPE:	Hardy perennial.
DESCRIPTION:	Fennel can grow to 1.5 metres/5 feet. It has green feathery fronds, finely-cut leaves and yellow flowers in late summer.
CONDITIONS:	Sun in a moist soil.
HOW TO GROW:	Sow directly in the garden in late spring, then thin out to 30 cm/12 inches apart. Replant side shoots and rooted pieces from plants in late spring or divide established roots in autumn. Do not plant near beans, caraway, tomatoes, kohlrabi or coriander (cilantro).
HOW TO PRESERVE:	Dry or freeze leaves and dry ripe seeds.
MAIN USES:	Fronds and seeds are used to give a mild aniseed flavour to pickles, biscuits, fish and pork dishes and liqueurs. A relative of fennel, Florence fennel, is grown for its bulb which is eaten as a cooked or salad vegetable.
MEDICINAL USES:	In gripe water, as an appetite stimulant, anti-flatulent and diuretic.

Feverfew

(tanacetum parthenium)

Feverfew is a member of the daisy family and one of the few aromatic herbs that bees dislike.

TYPE:	Hardy perennial.
DESCRIPTION:	Growing to about 45 cm/18 inches high, feverfew has deeply segmented yellow-green leaves and white daisy-like flowers which grow on tall stems in mid to late summer.
CONDITIONS:	Sun in a well-drained soil.
HOW TO GROW:	Sow in seed trays in early spring or directly in the garden, then thin to 30 cm/12 inches apart. Take stem cuttings in spring.
HOW TO PRESERVE:	Dry sprigs.
MAIN USES:	The leaves are sometimes used in salads or sandwiches but can cause local irritation.
MEDICINAL USES:	To treat migraine and tense headaches and to prevent or relieve insect bites.

ABOVE: Feverfew is often used in salads

Hyssop

(hyssopus officinalis)

Once considered holy and used for cleaning sacred sites, hyssop was a popular strewing herb in Medieval times as well as being used to make herbal tea and a kind of tobacco.

TYPE:	Hardy perennial.
DESCRIPTION:	A shrubby evergreen growing to about 60 cm/2 feet high, hyssop has narrow leaves and blue flowers towards the end of the summer.
CONDITIONS:	Sun or partial shade in a light, well-drained soil.
HOW TO GROW:	Take cuttings in spring for planting out in late summer or sow seeds in seed trays or directly in the garden in spring. Plant out 30 cm/12 inches apart. Trim back in autumn; hyssop can be close-clipped once established. Suitable for containers.
HOW TO PRESERVE:	Dry flowering sprigs in summer.
MAIN USES:	Used in pot-pourri or to garnish salads and vegetables. Hyssop oil is extracted commercially for perfumes.
MEDICINAL USES:	To combat coughs and catarrh and to reduce temperature.

LAVENDER

(lavendula angustifolia)

The name of this herb comes from the Latin word *lavare,* to wash, indicating that even ancient peoples valued this plant for its cleansing and cosmetic properties.

TYPE: Hardy or half-hardy perennial.

DESCRIPTION: A bushy plant up to 90 cm/3 feet high with long, pale green or greyish leaves and the familiar mauve or purple spikes of lavender flowers which attract bees and butterflies.

CONDITIONS: Sun in a well-drained, sandy soil.

HOW TO GROW: Take stem cuttings from side shoots in spring or autumn, then plant out 30 cm/12 inches apart. Prune in autumn after flowering to promote new growth in spring. Start new plants regularly as established plants can become straggly. Suitable for large containers.

HOW TO PRESERVE: Dry bunches of newly opened flowers. Save clippings for throwing on the coals at barbecues.

MAIN USES: Fresh leaves are used in fruit salads or punches or to flavour grilled meats but lavender is best known for its use in cosmetics, toiletries and lavender bags. It is also an effective moth repellent. Flowers can be crystallized for desserts.

MEDICINAL USES: An anti-depressant in aromatherapy and to lower blood pressure.

OPPOSITE: Hyssop has many and varied uses

Lemon Balm

(melissa officinalis)

The name of this aromatic herb means 'honey bee' in Greek and it was planted as a food for bees which still find it irresistible. Its fragrant leaves were used as a strewing herb.

Type:	Hardy perennial.
Description:	Looking a little like mint, lemon balm forms a dense clump about 60 cm/2 feet high. The nettle-shaped leaves are pale greeny yellow and lemon scented. White or pink flowers appear up the stem from mid to late summer.
Conditions:	Sun in a moist, rich soil.
How to grow:	Take stem cuttings in late spring or summer and plant out the following spring 30 cm/12 inches apart, or divide clumps in spring. Can also be sewn in seed trays in late spring, without covering then planted out, although lemon balm is slow to germinate. Suitable for large containers.
How to preserve:	Dry or freeze leaves.
Main uses:	Leaves are used for their lemon fragrance in stuffings, salad dressings, preserves or wine cups. Lemon balm was the main ingredient in *eau-des-carmes,* the forerunner of *eau-de-Cologne* and is used in pot-pourri.
Medicinal uses:	To treat fever, poor digestion, nausea and vomiting.

Lovage

(levisticum officinale)

Lovage was grown in monastic gardens as a cure for many diseases. It has a taste similar to celery.

Type:	Hardy perennial.
Description:	The tall stems of lovage can grow over 90 cm/3 feet. The large leaves are similar to parsley and the sulphur-yellow flowers bloom in mid summer.
Conditions:	Sun or partial shade in a rich soil.
How to grow:	Lift existing plants in spring and replant side shoots 90 cm/3 feet apart. Sow in pots in mid to late summer, keep moist, then plant out in autumn or spring. Lovage dies back in winter.
How to preserve:	Dry ripe seeds and young leaves. Dry roots in autumn.
Main uses:	Fresh or dried leaves give a nutty flavour to soups, stews and salads.
Medicinal uses:	An aid to digestion, to treat colic and dyspepsia, as an antiseptic gargle for tonsillitis or as an antiseptic for wounds.

Marjoram

(origanum majorana)

An ancient symbol of youth, beauty and happiness, there are many varieties of marjoram and oregano, which is of the same family. The flavour varies depending on the climate and oregano grown in warmer areas has a stronger flavour.

Type:	Tender perennial; treat as half-hardy annual.
Description:	A tender plant about 30 cm/12 inches high, marjoram has small grey-green leaves and clumps of pale cream or pink flowers in late summer.
Conditions:	Sun in a well-drained, rich soil.
How to grow:	Sow in seed trays in spring, then plant out 15 cm/6 inches apart. Suitable for containers.
How to preserve:	Dry or freeze leaves.
Main uses:	Use fresh or dried for flavouring soups, egg or vegetable dishes, casseroles or stuffings. Oregano is especially popular in Italian cooking. Marjoram and oregano are also used in pot-pourri.
Medicinal uses:	Externally to treat bruises and strains.

OPPOSITE: Marjoram used in soups and casseroles

MINT

PEPPERMINT (mentha piperita) and SPEARMINT (mentha spicata)

Peppermint is mainly used as a flavouring and for drinks, while spearmint is the mint used for flavouring potatoes and making mint sauce. All varieties are easy to grow.

TYPE: Hardy perennial.

DESCRIPTION: All mints are vigorous herbs growing to about 60 cm/2 feet with dark green, oval, glossy leaves and spikes of lilac flowers in mid summer which attract butterflies. Some varieties have variegated or more rounded, downy leaves.

CONDITIONS: Partial shade in a rich soil.

HOW TO GROW: Lift plants in spring or early summer and replant rooted pieces 30 cm/12 inches apart. Mint can be invasive and is particularly suitable for containers.

HOW TO PRESERVE: Freeze or dry leaves or store in oil or vinegar.

MAIN USES: Peppermint is used as a flavouring in confectionery, a garnish for drinks and for peppermint tea. Spearmint is used to flavour vegetables and fruits, in stuffings and as an ingredient in mint sauce, chutneys or mayonnaise.

MEDICINAL USES: An aid to digestion and to combat indigestion, nausea, insomnia, anxiety and dizziness.

Parsley

(petroselinum crispum)

Brought to Britain by the Romans, parsley is indigenous to the Middle East and North Africa. Pliny thought it the most important medicinal herb.

Type:	Hardy biennial; treat as annual.
Description:	Dark green, curled leaves grow in clusters on the plant which reaches a height of about 30 cm/ 12 inches. The small flowers are greenish yellow or white.
Conditions:	Sun or partial shade on the roots in a rich soil.
How to grow:	Soak seeds in water for 24 hours to speed up slow germination, then make successive sowings in seed trays in late spring and plant out 45 cm/18 inches apart. Suitable for containers.
How to preserve:	Freeze leaves.
Main uses:	The most widely known culinary herb in the world, parsley is used in *bouquet garni* and *fines herbes* and as a flavouring for an enormous variety of savoury foods.
Medicinal uses:	A general tonic, diuretic and anti-rheumatic and to combat liver complaints, jaundice, dropsy and urinary stones.

ABOVE: Mints are very versatile

Rosemary

(rosmarinus officinalis)

Despite its Mediterranean origins, rosemary flourishes in temperate areas. It is the herb of remembrance and the Ancient Greeks wove sprigs into their hair to improve their memories. Rosemary sprigs were woven into bridal bouquets as reminders of fidelity.

Type:	Hardy perennial.
Description:	A woody, evergreen bush about 90 cm/3 feet high, rosemary has pale grey-green, spiky leaves which are highly aromatic. The pale lilac-blue, delicate flowers shroud the whole bush in summer.
Conditions:	Sun and shelter from winds in a sandy, well-drained soil.
How to grow:	Take stem cuttings, pinch out the tops, then plant out 90 cm/3 feet apart. Trim regularly. Suitable for containers.
How to preserve:	Freeze or dry leaves for pot-pourri; it is best to use fresh for cooking. Save prunings and woody stems for barbecues.
Main uses:	Pot-pourri, shampoos and hair preparations are the main uses of rosemary. In cooking, it may be used to flavour lamb, pork or chicken, or be added to puddings and sorbets.
Medicinal uses:	To combat gastric problems, tension, nervous headaches and depression.

OPPOSITE: A very rewarding herb, rosemary has many uses

Rue

(ruta graveolens)

The herb of grace has long been highly regarded in herbal medicine throughout Europe. A native of the Mediterranean, it was brought to Britain by the Romans and then taken to the United States. Used to prevent the spread of infection, judges used to have a bunch in front of them during court appearances.

TYPE:	Hardy perennial.
DESCRIPTION:	With distinctive, blue-green, long, rounded leaves, rue can grow to a woody shrub over 60 cm/2 feet tall. Its yellow flowers appear in summer.
CONDITIONS:	Sun and shelter from winds in a well-drained soil.
HOW TO GROW:	Take stem cuttings in summer or sow seed in trays in early spring, then plant out 30 cm/12 inches apart. Cut back established plants in spring.
HOW TO PRESERVE:	Use fresh.
MAIN USES:	Used sparingly in egg, cheese or fish dishes, rue yields medicinal oils commercially. The leaves are used to flavour liqueurs.
MEDICINAL USES:	A nerve tonic, to treat nervous headaches, bites and stings. Rue is highly toxic in large doses.

OPPOSITE: Rue has a well established medicinal association

SAGE

(salvia officinalis)

An easy herb to grow and very useful in the kitchen, sage brightens the herb garden throughout the year. It has been used medicinally since Ancient Roman times as a universal panacea.

TYPE: Hardy perennial.

DESCRIPTION: Sage grows to a woody bush about 60 cm/2 feet high with oval, green-grey, soft leaves which are slightly wrinkled; some varieties are variegated, while others have purple leaves. Its purple-blue flowers appear in mid summer and attract bees.

CONDITIONS: Sun in a well-drained, alkaline soil.

HOW TO GROW: Take stem cuttings with a heel in spring and provide heat from below, or pin down side shoots in spring, cover with soil, then divide when rooted. Trim back regularly and replace plants every few years, otherwise they become leggy and woody.

HOW TO PRESERVE: Dry or freeze leaves or preserve in oil or vinegar.

MAIN USES: Used in stuffings, particularly with rich, fatty foods such as pork or duck, sage is an aid to digestion. Fresh leaves can be dipped in egg white and fried.

MEDICINAL USES: Good for the digestion, anti-flatulent and used to combat laryngitis, tonsillitis and other kinds of sore throat.

Salad Burnet

(poterium sanguisorba)

Once regarded as a herb which would prevent the plague, there has been a recent resurgence in the popularity of salad burnet as a garden herb.

TYPE:	Hardy perennial.
DESCRIPTION:	A bushy plant, salad burnet has dense rosettes of leaves from which stems of small, serrated leaves spray out like wings. The small red flowers bloom in mid summer.
CONDITIONS:	Full sun in any soil.
HOW TO GROW:	Sow in seed trays in spring or outside when warmer, then plant out 30 cm/12 inches apart; will often self-seed. Divide roots in autumn. Cut off flowers to encourage leaf growth.
HOW TO PRESERVE:	Dry leaves.
MAIN USES:	Salad burnet is used in spring salads and wine cups or to flavour or garnish cream cheese.
MEDICINAL USES:	As an astringent to heal wounds and to treat gout and rheumatism.

NEXT PAGE: Sage long recognised as an aid to digestion

St John's Wort

(hypericum perforatum)

Once used to exorcise evil spirits, St John's wort is an easy herb to grow.

Type:	Hardy perennial.
Description:	The leaves of St John's wort appear to be spotted with black because of oil glands beneath the surface. Throughout the summer bright yellow flowers bloom on tall stems about 90 cm/3 feet high.
Conditions:	Sun and shelter from winds in any soil.
How to grow:	Sow in seed trays in early spring, then plant out 20 cm/8 inches apart, or take stem cuttings in spring.
How to preserve:	Dry flowers or leaves or preserve in oil or vinegar.
Main uses:	St John's wort is mainly a medicinal herb.
Medicinal uses:	To treat wounds, bruising, haemorrhoids and sciatica, also as a mouthwash and to combat coughs and neuralgia.

Savory, Summer

(satureia hortensis)

Savory used to be rubbed on bee stings for pain relief and Virgil always planted savory near his bee hives as it improved the flavour of the honey. Winter savory (*satureia montana*) is a similar perennial which used to be taken as an aphrodisiac.

Type:	Hardy annual.
Description:	Very attractive to bees and butterflies, savory has tiny, pointed leaves and subtle pinky-white flowers in mid summer which grow up the stem. It grows about 45 cm/18 inches tall.
Conditions:	Sun in any soil.
How to grow:	Sow in seed trays in early spring or directly in the garden when warmer, then plant out 23 cm/ 9 inches apart.
How to preserve:	Dry leaves.
Main uses:	Used to flavour vegetables, meats and poultry, savory also makes a pleasant herb tea.
Medicinal uses:	To combat flatulence, diarrhoea and nervous disorders and as an expectorant.

Sorrel

(rumex acetosa)

Sorrel is thought by some to be the original shamrock, chosen by St Patrick to illustrate the Holy Trinity. Often used as a salad ingredient in Europe.

Type:	Hardy perennial.
Description:	The large, succulent leaves of sorrel are rather like spinach leaves. Red and orange flowers grow on tall spikes in summer and attract goldfinches and greenfinches. The plant is about 60 cm/2 feet high.
Conditions:	Sun with shaded roots in a well-nourished, moist soil.
How to grow:	Sow directly in the garden in early spring, then thin out to 30 cm/12 inches apart. Divide roots of existing plants in early spring and replant. Sorrel can be invasive. Cut off flower heads and pick leaves regularly to maintain supply.
How to preserve:	Freeze leaves.
Main uses:	Sorrel can be used in soups, as a vegetable like spinach or in sauces and marinades. As a garnish, add to hot dishes at the last moment.
Medicinal uses:	As a laxative and to treat boils, eczema and acne.

SWEET CICELY

(myrrhis odorata)

A highly aromatic herb with the subtle scent of liquorice, sweet cicely is native to Britain and has always been popular among herbalists.

TYPE:	Hardy perennial.
DESCRIPTION:	Soft, bright green, fern-like leaves are contrasted by white umbels of flowers in spring. Sweet cicely grows to a height of about 60 cm/2 feet.
CONDITIONS:	Sun or partial shade in a slightly moist soil.
HOW TO GROW:	Sow seeds directly in the garden in autumn or plant out self-sown seedlings. Divide roots in autumn or early spring and replant 30 cm/12 inches apart.
HOW TO PRESERVE:	Dry ripe seeds.
MAIN USES:	Use fresh leaves or seeds to add a natural sweetness to salads, fruit, fruit compotes, mousses and ice cream.
MEDICINAL USES:	As an expectorant and anti-flatulent and to reduce high blood pressure.

ABOVE: Herbs have a long established reputation for medicinal properties

TANSY

(tanacetum vulgare)

Once used as an embalming agent and to preserve meat, tansy is one of the bitter herbs of Passover and flavours Easter cakes.

TYPE:	Hardy perennial.
DESCRIPTION:	Highly aromatic, tansy has dark green, feathery, fern-like leaves and bright yellow flowers throughout the summer.
CONDITIONS:	Sun in any soil.
HOW TO GROW:	Divide plants and plant out 30 cm/12 inches apart. Lift plants and cut back roots as it can be invasive.
HOW TO PRESERVE:	Dry leaves or flowers.
MAIN USES:	Dried sprays of tansy flowers are used in arrangements. The leaves are an ingredient in moth repellent mixtures.
MEDICINAL USES:	Used to treat scabies, gout and worms, tansy is contra-indicated in pregnancy.

TARRAGON

(artemisia dracunculus)

Both French and Russian tarragon are available, but the French has the best flavour. The Latin name means 'little dragon', a description of the brown, coiled roots. The common name derives from the French translation, *estragon*. It has been used for thousands of years as a antidote for snake bites.

TYPE:	Hardy perennial.
DESCRIPTION:	Growing up to 60 cm/2 feet high, tarragon has long, spiky leaves and insignificant yellow flowers in mid summer.
CONDITIONS:	Sun in a light soil.
HOW TO GROW:	Take stem cuttings or divide roots of established plants and plant out 23 cm/9 inches apart. Cut back in autumn and protect from frosts, or bring inside in winter. Start new plants every four years for the best flavour. Suitable for containers.
HOW TO PRESERVE:	Freeze, dry or store leaves in oil or vinegar.
MAIN USES:	Used in fines herbes and many classic sauces such as hollandaise, béarnaise and tartare, tarragon is also good with shellfish and chicken dishes.
MEDICINAL USES:	An anti-oxidant, tarragon is good for the stomach and is used to combat distension and flatulence.

THYME

(thymus vulgaris)

Believed to be one of the herbs used for the baby Jesus' bedding, thyme is often included in cribs at Christmas time. In Ancient Greece, it was used as a symbol of elegance.

TYPE:	Hardy perennial.
DESCRIPTION:	Thyme grows in clumps about 20 cm/8 inches high. The tiny leaves can be dark, dusty green, golden or variegated. Small, pale flowers appear in early summer to attract bees and butterflies.
CONDITIONS:	Sun in a light, well-drained soil.
HOW TO GROW:	Sow in seed trays, then plant out 25 cm/10 inches apart or take stem cuttings before flowering. Suitable for containers.
HOW TO PRESERVE:	Dry or freeze sprigs or preserve in oil.
MAIN USES:	An essential ingredient in bouquet garni, thyme is also used for stuffings, roast dishes and rich meat casseroles. Oil of thyme is used for perfumes.
MEDICINAL USES:	An expectorant, antiseptic and antibacterial, also used as a gargle to ease sore throats.

INDEX